HENRY GOES WEST

To librarians, parents, and teachers:

Henry Goes West is a Parents Magazine READ ALOUD Original — one title in a series of colorfully illustrated and fun-to-read stories that young readers will be sure to come back to time and time again.

Now, in this special school and library edition of *Henry Goes West,* adults have an even greater opportunity to increase children's responsiveness to reading and learning — and to have fun every step of the way.

When you finish this story, check the special section at the back of the book. There you will find games, projects, things to talk about, and other educational activities designed to make reading enjoyable by giving children and adults a chance to play together, work together, and talk over the story they have just read.

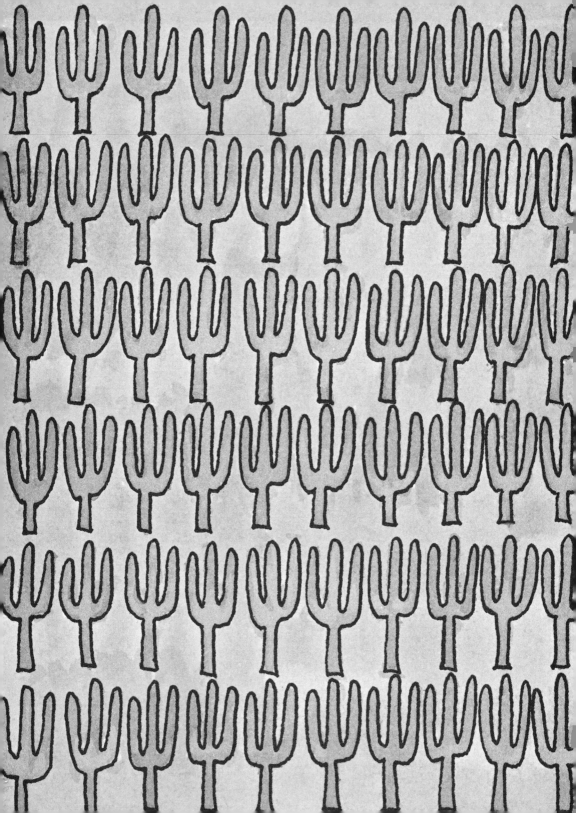

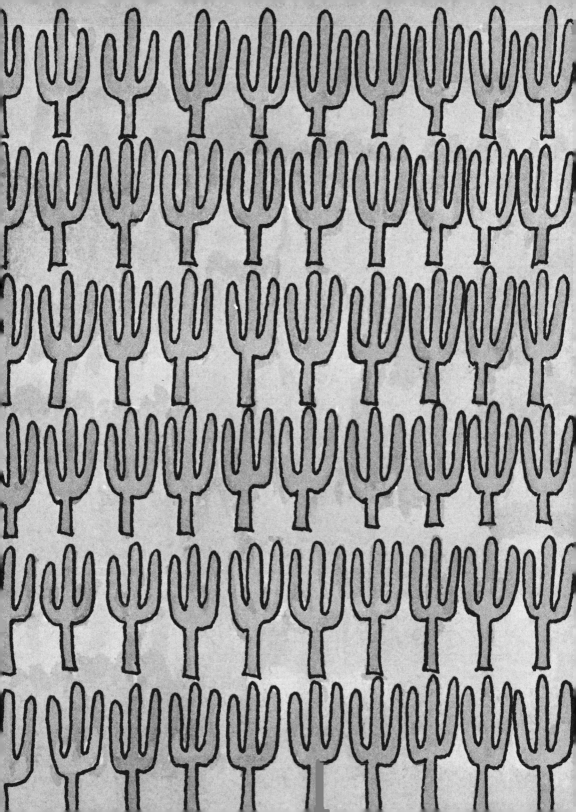

For a free color catalog describing Gareth Stevens' list of high-quality books, call 1-800-542-2595 (USA) or 1-800-461-9120 (Canada). Gareth Stevens' Fax: (414) 225-0377.

Parents Magazine READ ALOUD Originals:

A Garden for Miss Mouse
Aren't You Forgetting
  Something, Fiona?
Bicycle Bear
The Biggest Shadow in
  the Zoo
Bread and Honey
Buggly Bear's Hiccup Cure
But No Elephants
Cats! Cats! Cats!
The Clown-Arounds
The Clown-Arounds Go
  on Vacation
Elephant Goes to School
The Fox with Cold Feet
Get Well, Clown-Arounds!
The Ghost in Dobbs Diner
The Giggle Book
The Goat Parade
Golly Gump Swallowed a Fly
Henry Babysits

Henry Goes West
Henry's Awful Mistake
Henry's Important Date
The Housekeeper's Dog
The Little Witch Sisters
The Man Who Cooked
  for Himself
Milk and Cookies
Miss Mopp's Lucky Day
No Carrots for Harry!
Oh, So Silly!
The Old Man and the
  Afternoon Cat
One Little Monkey
The Peace-and-Quiet Diner
Pets I Wouldn't Pick
Pickle Things
Pigs in the House
Rabbit's New Rug
Rupert, Polly, and Daisy
Sand Cake

Septimus Bean and His
  Amazing Machine
Sheldon's Lunch
Sherlock Chick and the
  Giant Egg Mystery
Sherlock Chick's First Case
The Silly Tail Book
Snow Lion
Socks for Supper
Sweet Dreams, Clown-
  Arounds!
Ten Furry Monsters
There's No Place Like Home
This Farm is a Mess
Those Terrible Toy-Breakers
Up Goes Mr. Downs
The Very Bumpy Bus Ride
Where's Rufus?
Who Put the Pepper in
  the Pot?
Witches Four

Library of Congress Cataloging-in-Publication Data

Quackenbush, Robert M.
    Henry goes West / by Robert Quackenbush.
        p. cm. -- (Parents magazine read aloud original)
    "North American library edition"--T.p. verso.
    Summary: Lonely without his friend Clara who is vacationing out West, Henry the Duck decides to pay her a surprise visit.
    ISBN 0-8368-0996-3
    [1. Ducks--Fiction. 2. West (U.S.)--Fiction. 3. Humorous stories.] I. Title. II. Series.
PZ7.Q16Hc 1994
[E]--dc20   94-11353

This North American library edition published in 1994 by Gareth Stevens Publishing, 1555 North RiverCenter Drive, Suite 201, Milwaukee, Wisconsin, 53212, USA, under an arrangement with Pages, Inc., St. Petersburg, Florida.

Text and illustrations © 1982 by Robert Quackenbush. Portions of end matter adapted from material first published in the newsletter *From Parents to Parents* by the Parents Magazine Read Aloud Book Club, © 1988 by Gruner + Jahr, USA, Publishing; other portions © 1994 by Gareth Stevens, Inc.

Printed in the United States of America

1 2 3 4 5 6 7 8 9 99 98 97 96 95 94

HENRY GOES WEST

by Robert Quackenbush

GARETH STEVENS PUBLISHING • MILWAUKEE

PARENTS MAGAZINE PRESS • NEW YORK

For Piet

A Parents Magazine
Read Aloud Original

Henry the Duck missed
his friend Clara,
who was vacationing out West.
He decided to pay her
a surprise visit.
So he packed his bag
and took the first plane
heading West to meet her.

Henry arrived at
Clara's guest ranch
early the next morning.
But the ranch was closed.
Everyone had just left
for an all-day trail ride.
They would not be back
until midnight.

Henry decided to
have a look around
the ranch while he
waited for Clara.
As he was snapping a picture
near the barn,
Henry backed right into a mule.

The surprised mule
kicked Henry!
Henry landed on
the back of a horse.

16

The horse was a
bucking bronco!
Henry was taken
for a wild ride.
Then he was tossed
over a fence.

Henry landed in a bull's pen!
The bull chased Henry.
Henry ran and ran.

At last Henry got out
of the bull's pen.
He went to sit
on a large rock.
But he did not see
the cactus behind it.
Henry sat down
on the cactus!

Henry jumped up
and quacked loudly.
The noise frightened
some cattle
grazing nearby.

The cattle began running.
Soon they were racing
at full speed.
Henry had started
a stampede!

Henry escaped to the hills
in the nick of time.
He pulled the
cactus stickers
from his tail.
Then he headed
back to the ranch.

On the way, Henry
spotted an unusual rock.
He thought it would make
a good present for Clara.
But as soon as he
picked up the rock...

he heard a loud rumbling
from the mountaintop.
Henry had started
a landslide!
He ran as fast as
he could go.

Henry got clear
of the landslide.
Then he went straight back
to the ranch
to wait for Clara.

Henry waited and waited.
It was turning cold
on the desert.
So Henry built a campfire.
He stood close to the fire
to warm his tail feathers.
Too close.

Suddenly, Henry's
tail feathers
began to sizzle!
He made a beeline
for the water
and dove in.

Henry was soaking wet
and all worn out.
He wished Clara would hurry up
and get there.

At last the riding party returned.
But Clara was not with them.
Henry asked one of the cowboys
if he had seen her.

"Sorry, mister," said
the cowboy...

"Clara went home yesterday.
She said she was lonesome
for someone named Henry."

Notes to Grown-ups

Major Themes

Here is a quick guide to the significant themes and concepts at work in *Henry Goes West*:

- Look before you leap – not doing so led Henry into a series of problems.
- The importance of letting people know where you are – as Henry should have done.

Step-by-step Ideas for Reading and Talking

Here are some ideas for further give-and-take between grown-ups and children. The following topics encourage creative discussion of *Henry Goes West* and invite the kind of open-ended response that is consistent with many contemporary approaches to reading, including Whole Language:

- Henry should have told Clara that he was heading west to see her. In the punch line at the end, Clara told someone where she was going so Henry knew where to find her. The vital lesson for your child is to tell the people at home before going off to visit a friend, even if the friend only lives upstairs or just over the fence. With this story, you can remind your youngster without alarming her or him.
- Read the story a page or two at a time with a pause to ask, "What do you think will happen next?" Your child might enjoy trying to outguess the author and perhaps suggest even more mayhem than is in the book.
- Robert Quackenbush has written a number of stories about Henry the Duck. What kind of stories might be written by an author named James Oinkles? Mary Mooe? Can you and your child together make up any other author-animal combinations?

Games for Learning

Games and activities can stimulate young readers and listeners alike to find out more about words, numbers, and ideas. Here are more ideas for turning learning into fun:

What Came Next?

Henry's adventures follow a familiar and well-loved children's theme — a chain reaction of mostly harmless misadventures. You can play a cause-and-effect game with your child that will reinforce sequencing skills as you review the chain of events in this book.

Print the first sentence of each set below on the top half of a sheet of paper. Print the second sentence on the bottom. Cut each piece of paper in half, using simple and irregular cuts so the two parts of each "puzzle" fit together. Spread the bottom pieces out on a table or the floor. Pick one of the top halves and read its sentence aloud. By reading or matching the puzzle shapes, ask your child to find the piece that tells what happened next. Your child may give you the answer in his or her words and may need help reading the sentences and locating the matching piece.

Sentence Sets:

Henry backed into a mule. The mule kicked Henry.
Henry landed on a horse. The horse tossed Henry over
the fence.
Henry landed in the bull's pen. The bull chased Henry.
Henry sat on a cactus and quacked loudly. The cattle got
scared and started to stampede.
Henry picked up a rock. Henry started a landslide.
Henry sat by the fire to warm up. Henry's feathers
caught fire.

This "What Came Next?" game also stresses visual discrimination, as your child can locate and match the puzzle pieces by shape.

Picture Postcards

Have your child look at the postcard that Henry received from Clara at the beginning of this book. See if your child can tell you what things most postcards have in common. If possible, look together at postcards that your family has received. Then encourage your child to make a postcard, using pictures found in magazines that are then glued onto an index card. Ask your child questions about the card (for example, "Where is this card from? What message would you write? To whom would you send the card?").

About the Author/Artist

When ROBERT QUACKENBUSH manages to get away from the city, he usually finds himself on what he calls a "Henry-the-Duck vacation." That means his plane flight is cancelled, his hotel forgets to keep his room for him, and it rains every single day. But Mr. Quackenbush has that rare ability to turn a disaster into a funny story.

Mr. Quackenbush is the author/artist of more than one hundred books for children. He has been awarded honors and prizes, and recently was nominated for the Edgar Allen Poe Award in the juvenile category. His artwork has been exhibited in leading museums across the United States and is now on display in the gallery he owns and runs in New York City. He also teaches writing and illustrating there.

Mr. Quackenbush, who is a native of Arizona, lives in New York City with his wife, Margery, and their son, Piet.

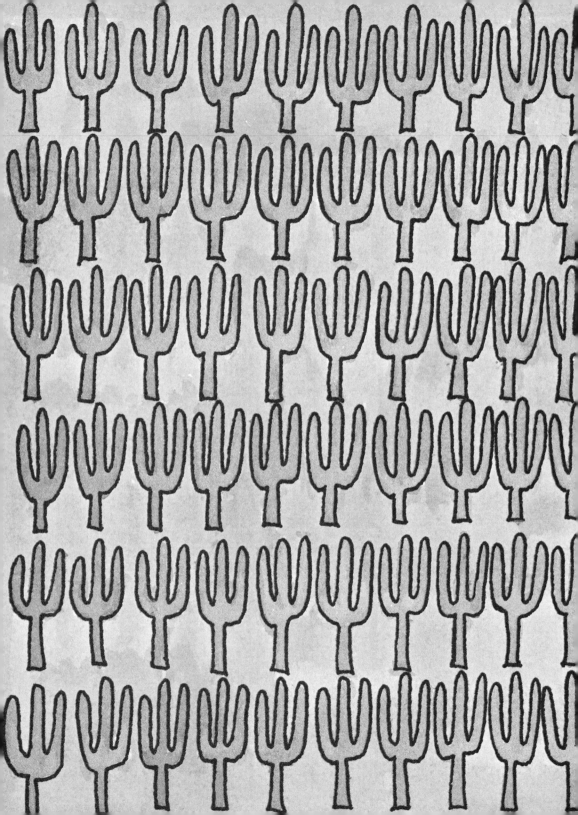

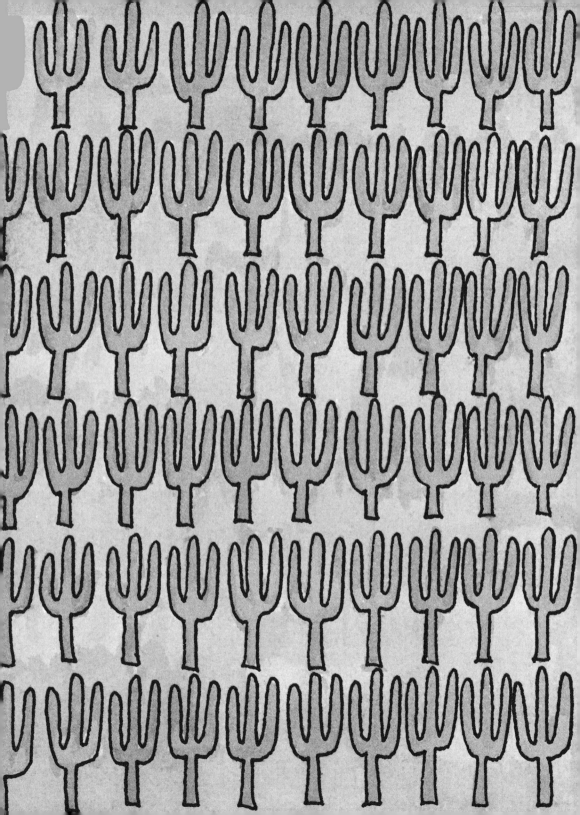